LAST REMAINS

— COMPANION —

Norman Osborn, formerly the Green Goblin, went from inmate to administrator at Ravencroft Institute, until the Sin-Eater cleansed him of his sins. Now he has to face everything he's done. He claims that the true threat behind the Sin-Eater — the mysterious villain Kindred — is really his son, Harry.

Meanwhile, Peter's Spider-Friends are in trouble. Known as the Order of the Web, they were helping Peter against the Sin-Eater when they were consumed by all the sins cleansed by the Sin-Eater and turned into demonic versions of themselves. Now they are Kindred's puppets with which he plans to wreak havoc on Spider-Man and the rest of New York City...

SPIDER-MAN CREATED BY STAN LEE & STEVE DITKO

COLLECTION EDITOR JENNIFER GRÜNWALD
ASSISTANT EDITOR DANIEL KIRCHHOFFER ✦ ASSISTANT MANAGING EDITOR MAIA LOY
ASSISTANT MANAGING EDITOR LISA MONTALBANO ✦ VP PRODUCTION & SPECIAL PROJECTS JEFF YOUNGQUIST
BOOK DESIGNERS ADAM DEL RE WITH JAY BOWEN
SVP PRINT, SALES & MARKETING DAVID GABRIEL ✦ EDITOR IN CHIEF C.B. CEBULSKI

the AMAZING SPIDER-MAN

LAST REMAINS COMPANION

WRITERS	**NICK SPENCER** & **MATTHEW ROSENBERG**

AMAZING SPIDER-MAN #50.LR-52.LR

ARTIST	**FEDERICO VICENTINI**
COLOR ARTISTS	**MARCIO MENYZ** WITH **ERICK ARCINIEGA** (#52.LR)

AMAZING SPIDER-MAN #53.LR-54.LR

PENCILERS	**FEDERICO VICENTINI** & **TAKESHI MIYAZAWA**
INKERS	**FEDERICO VICENTINI** & **TAKESHI MIYAZAWA** WITH **SCOTT HANNA**
COLOR ARTISTS	**MARCIO MENYZ** (#53.LR) & **ERICK ARCINIEGA** (#53.LR-54.LR)

LETTERERS	**VC's JOE CARAMAGNA** (#50.LR) & **ARIANA MAHER** (#51.LR-54.LR)
COVER ART	**SARA PICHELLI** & **RACHELLE ROSENBERG** (#50.LR), **MARCELO FERREIRA** & **DAVID CURIEL** (#51.LR-54.LR)

ASSISTANT EDITORS TOM GRONEMAN & LINDSEY COHICK
ASSOCIATE EDITOR KATHLEEN WISNESKI
EDITOR NICK LOWE

"--STARING RIGHT BACK AT ME."

I *UNDERSTAND* NOW. I SOLD MY SOUL TO A *DEMON*.

I LET IT TURN ME INTO A MONSTER THAT DESTROYED *COUNTLESS* LIVES. AND ALL I ASKED FOR IN EXCHANGE--

--WAS TO BE FREE OF THE *GUILT*.

OH, COME ON, NORMAN--

--YOU'RE HARDLY THE FIRST TO BLAME A *DIVINE POWER* FOR YOUR OWN SHORTCOMINGS. AND YOU'RE CERTAINLY AMONG THE LEAST CONVINCING.

I CAME BACK TO RAVENCROFT AND TRIED TO GIVE YOU A CHANCE. I THOUGHT PERHAPS WE COULD DO SOME *GOOD* TOGETHER.

BUT NOW I SEE YOU HAVEN'T CHANGED AT *ALL.* WHATEVER IT IS YOU WERE PLANNING DOWN IN THOSE HIDDEN SUBLEVELS, I'M SURE THE AUTHORITIES WOULD LIKE TO HEAR ABOUT IT.

THE ONLY REASON I HAVEN'T REPORTED IT YET IS YOUR INSISTENCE THAT LIVES ARE AT *IMMEDIATE RISK.* BUT I WON'T SIT HERE AND LISTEN TO YOU TRY TO PASS THE BLAME FOR--

YOU *MISUNDERSTAND* ME, DOCTOR KAFKA...

I BLAME ONLY *MYSELF.*

I'M THE ONE WHO IS R-R-RESPONSIBLE. RESPONSIBLE FOR...FOR...

--WHILE THEY ARE MOST DEFINITELY TRYING TO HURT ME.

GWEN, COME ON--NFF--YOU HAVE TO FIGHT THIS...

OH, PLEASE--NOT THE OLD "TRY TO GET THROUGH TO THEM" ROUTINE.

I PROMISE YOU THEY'RE LONG GONE.

WHAM

BUT I CAN READ YOU LOUD AND CLEAR.

--BACK IN YOUR... LAIR, OR WHAT HAVE YOU. YOU SAID YOU KNEW WHO WAS *RESPONSIBLE* FOR ALL THIS--THE *SIN-EATER*, THE ATTACK ON *RAVENCROFT*.

YOU REFERRED TO THIS PERSON AS--

"--KINDRED."

A NAME I'LL CONFESS I'M NOT FAMILIAR WITH.

BUT THEN-- AND YOU WERE CONSIDERABLY DISORIENTED AND FRANTIC AT THIS POINT, SO I'LL FORGIVE YOU IF YOU MISSPOKE-- BUT YOU SAID HE WAS YOUR--

SON.

I SAID HE WAS MY SON.

"MY HARRY."

HE WAS *HERE*, YOU KNOW.

"HE VISITED ME WHEN I WAS STILL A PATIENT HERE. LOCKED AWAY IN A CELL WHERE I BELONGED.

"I COULD'VE TRIED TO TALK TO HIM. HELP HIM. STOP HIM FROM DOING ALL OF THIS. BUT WHAT DID I DO INSTEAD?

"I *TAUNTED* HIM."

I CAN'T STOP SEEING ALL THE THINGS I DID TO HIM. THE INSULTS, THE BETRAYALS, THE ABUSE.

AND SO MUCH *WORSE*. I PUT HIM THROUGH SO MUCH... THINGS A FATHER SHOULD NEVER DO TO A SON.

EVERYTHING HE HAS BECOME IS A REFLECTION OF ME AND MY OWN EVIL.

THE SINS OF THE FATHER, THE SINS OF THE SON. I CAN NO LONGER EVEN TELL WHERE ONE ENDS AND THE OTHER BEGINS.

AND WHAT'S EVEN WORSE--

YOU LOOK *EXHAUSTED.* BUT THEN, I GET IT.

ACTUALLY MANAGING TO KEEP YOUR "LOVED" ONES ALIVE IS HARD WORK.

PROBABLY WHY YOU'VE ALWAYS *SUCKED* AT IT.

SORRY. THAT WAS *UNFAIR.*

I KNOW THAT KIND OF THING *GNAWS* AT YOU.

ANYA, WAIT--

NO! NO-- WAIT--

I'VE NEVER FELT LIKE THIS BEFORE. SO POWERLESS.

BUT I HAVE TO DO SOMETHING. I HAVE TO--

THAT'S ENOUGH, NORMAN.

I'VE SPENT A CAREER TRYING TO HELP THE ONES EVERYONE ELSE SAID WERE TOO FAR GONE. IT EVENTUALLY COST ME MY LIFE.*

BUT I'M NOT GOING TO LET THAT STOP ME.

IF YOU'RE TRULY SINCERE IN WANTING TO MAKE THIS RIGHT, I MIGHT HAVE AN IDEA. BUT IT WON'T BE EASY.

ANYTHING-- I'LL DO ANYTHING.

*DR. KAFKA WAS KILLED BACK SUPERIOR SPIDEY #5 (AND BROUGH BACK DURING THE CLONE CONSPIRAC) --LITERATI LINDSE

YOU SAY YOUR SON WON'T LISTEN TO YOU. THAT'S NOT AN UNUSUAL PROBLEM AT ALL.

IN CASES OF RECONCILIATION AFTER SEVERE FAMILY TRAUMA, IT CAN OFTEN BE HELPFUL TO HAVE A SORT OF BUFFER BETWEEN THE TWO PARTIES--

--AN INTERMEDIARY.

SOMEONE WHO CAN BE SEEN AS A FAIR ARBITER WHO CAN HELP NEGOTIATE THROUGH ALL THE HISTORY AND HURT.

AND YOU... WOULD DO THIS?

I COULD TRY, BUT I SUSPECT GIVEN YOUR SON'S STATE, HE MIGHT RESPOND BETTER--

--TO SOMEONE HE ALREADY KNOWS.

SO ASK YOURSELF, NORMAN--WHO MIGHT INTERCEDE ON YOUR BEHALF?

IF HARRY WOULD NEVER LISTEN TO YOU, WHO WOULD HE LISTEN TO? WHO COULD GET THROUGH TO HIM?

...WHERE IS SPIDER-MAN?

YEAH, IT'S A FAIR QUESTION--

--AND YOU'D THINK I'D HAVE AN ANSWER.

AFTER ALL, ME AND MY EX HAVE BEEN BUSY REBUILDING OUR FRIENDSHIP--

--EVER SINCE HE RE-REVEALED HIS SECRET IDENTITY TO ME.

THEN THERE WAS ALL THAT UGLY BUSINESS WITH KRAVEN THE HUNTER IN CENTRAL PARK FOR US TO DEAL WITH TOGETHER.

I GUESS THAT REBUILT OUR BONDS OF TRUST ENOUGH THAT HE FELT LIKE HE COULD COME TO ME--

--WHEN HE NEEDED A FAVOR.

AT THE TIME, I WAS HAPPY TO OBLIGE. BUT NOW? WELL--

--NO GOOD DEED GOES UNPUNISHED, RIGHT?

GOOD EVENING, MS. HARDY.

YES, I AM AWARE THAT THIS IS SUPPOSED TO BE A PROMOTIONAL VISIT.

BUT AS I MADE CLEAR WHEN I *AGREED* TO THIS, I AM GONNA NEED SOME PERSONAL TIME WHILE I'M HOME TO SEE--

CANDACE? YOU'RE BREAKING UP-- SORRY--

--RECEPTION IN MANHATTAN IS ALWAYS SUCH A NIGHTMARE.

YOU NEED TO USE MINE, MA'AM? STILL GOT FOUR BARS--

NO THANKS--

--HAPPY TO JUST ENJOY THE VIEW.

GOOD TO FINALLY BE BACK--

--EVEN IF IT IS LATER THAN I'D WANTED.

POOR TIGER. I KNOW I ALREADY RUINED ALL HIS BIG SURPRISES. PRETTY BAD FORM--

--ESPECIALLY GIVEN HOW GOOD I'VE BEEN AT KEEPING *MINE*.

THIS PROMO TRIP WAS JUST AN EXCUSE TO COME HOME AND FINALLY TELL HIM THE TRUTH ABOUT WHAT I'VE BEEN UP TO IN HOLLYWOOD.

STILL PRETTY NERVOUS HOW HE'S GONNA TAKE THE NEWS THAT MY BIG COMEBACK MOVIE IS BEING DIRECTED BY... UH, *MYSTERIO.*

FEELS LIKE HE MIGHT NOT BE OKAY WITH THAT. THEN AGAIN, NOW MIGHT NOT BE A GOOD TIME TO 'FESS UP.

RAVENCROFT ERUPTS:

SPIDER-MAN, SIN-EATER and GREEN GOBLIN reported on scene, but WHO is on WHOSE side?!

OH, PETER, WHAT HAVE YOU GOTTEN YOURSELF INTO *THIS* TIME? RAVENCROFT MEANS *NORMAN OSBORN,* AND NORMAN OSBORN MEANS--

"I WILL *PROVE* MYSELF YOUR UNWAVERING DISCIPLE."

K-TRUNG

DO YOU HEAR ME, *MASTER?!* THOUGH YOU MAY CURSE ME BACK TO HELL, I WILL NOT STOP SERVING YOU!

YOU CHARGED ME WITH A GREAT AND GLORIOUS TASK-- A *WORLD* CLEANSED OF SIN.

--BUT I WILL NOT FAIL YOU AGAIN!

"NOW THEIR SINS BURN BRIGHTER THAN *EVER* BEFORE.

THRUMM

"SO I WILL ANSWER WITH RIGHTEOUS FIRE.

"MORLUN."

--OFF!

WAIT, PLEASE--PETER-- HE'S IN *GRAVE* DANGER!

YEAH, I KNOW. YOU'RE ALWAYS THE *CAUSE* OF IT.

NO--NO, YOU DON'T *UNDERSTAND.*

IT'S *HARRY.*

YOU'RE *LYING.*

I WISH I WERE...

YOU REALLY EXPECT ME TO BELIEVE THAT THE SIN-EATER JUST-- JUST *CURED* YOU OF YOUR--YOUR--

SINS. I CAN'T EXPLAIN IT.

NEITHER CAN I--

--BUT I CAN *CONFIRM* IT.

I'VE TREATED SEVERAL PATIENTS WHO HAVE BEEN "CLEANSED" BY STANLEY CARTER'S HAND. WHATEVER NORMAN OSBORN *USED* TO BE--

--HE'S NOT THAT ANYMORE.

YOU--YOU'RE ASHLEY KAFKA, AREN'T YOU?

I THOUGHT YOU WERE DEAD.

BACK AMONG THE LIVING, THANKFULLY.

WELL, NO OFFENSE, DOC, YOUR PSYCHIATRIC EXPERTISE COMES HIGHLY RECOMMENDED--BUT NO MATTER HOW MUCH EVIL YOU SAW SIN-EATER WIPE AWAY--

--SOME STAINS CAN *NEVER* REALLY COME OUT.

I--I UNDERSTAND WHY YOU HATE ME--I *DESERVE* IT--BUT, MAR[Y] JANE, YOU MUST BELIEVE ME--

--THIS ISN'T *ABOUT* ME. THIS IS ABOUT PETER. AND *HARRY.*

--AND IT PLEASES ME.

WHAT *IS* IT, SIR?

A BIOLOGICAL WEAPON. SOME TIME AGO, A MADWOMAN ATTEMPTED TO INFECT ALL OF MANHATTAN WITH IT--

--USING IT TO TURN THE INFECTED INTO SOMETHING TRULY TERRIFYING.

THE THREAT WAS ERADICATED, BUT A FEW VIALS OF THE AGENT WERE PRESERVED-- FOR RESEARCH PURPOSES.

SO... WHAT ARE *YOU* GONNA DO WITH IT?

USE IT FOR *BAIT*.

SBAM

I'M SO SORRY, ALL OF YOU. SUFFERING IS THE WAY OF THIS WORLD.

BUT KNOW THAT YOUR FAITH WILL BE *REWARDED*.

NOT IN THIS LIFE--

--BUT IN THE NEXT.

*THAT MADWOMAN SIN-EATER MENTIONED WAS SPIDER-QUEEN AND THE WEAPON CAUSED SPIDER-ISLAND! --NEBBISH NICK

THE ONE THEY CALL *MORLUN* UNDERSTANDS SUFFERING AS WELL.

HE LOST HIS FAMILY TO THE *SPIDERS.** AND INSTEAD OF BEING LEFT TO *MOURN*--

*BACK IN *SPIDER-GEDDON!* --NL

--HE FELT THE CHAINS OF *BONDAGE*.

AND WHILE HE MANAGED TO BREAK FREE AT LAST--

--ALL HE HAS KNOWN SINCE IS *HUNGER*.

SO I HAVE PREPARED A FEAST FOR HIM. AND FOR ME...

MY GREATEST TEST.

NICE SKYLIGHT.

YOU SHOULD REALLY GET THAT FIXED.

≶SIGH≷

COULD SOMEONE EXPLAIN THIS PLAN TO ME AGAIN?

IT'S SIMPLE, REALLY.

YOU WERE GOING TO USE THIS-- THE HAND OF VISHANTI--TO FIND THE DEMON WHO POSSESSED US, USING PETER'S CONNECTION TO THE WEB OF LIFE AND DESTINY. BUT YOU RAN INTO A... COMPLICATION.

SO INSTEAD, NOW YOU CAN USE US TO TRACK HIM THROUGH THE SAME WEB ON THE ASTRAL PLANE.

IT IS AN ELEGANT SOLUTION...

I IMAGINE YOU'D THINK SO--

--YOU WERE GOING TO COME UP WITH IT A FEW MINUTES FROM NOW.

I FIGURED WE COULD SAVE THE TIME.

YOU KNOW, I DEAL WITH CLAIRVOYANTS AND PROPHECY ALL THE TIME, AND I STILL FIND YOUR METHODS INFURIATING.

TRUST ME, YOU'RE NOT THE ONLY ONE, SNAPE.

BUT IF THIS IS THE PLAN THAT GETS US DELIVERING SOME PAYBACK FOR WHAT THIS KINDRED GUY JUST MADE US DO, I AM IN.

I'D IMAGINE WE ALL ARE. GWEN. NO TWELVE ANGRY MEN ROUTINE THIS TIME, RIGHT?

OBVIOUSLY. WHAT MATTERS RIGHT NOW IS ENDING THIS.

THE REST WE CAN SORT OUT LATER.

GOOD.

I'LL HANDLE THIS.

LIKE ALWAYS.

HEY--

--IS *THAT* WHAT WE'RE LOOKING FOR?

INDEED. HURRY, BEFORE--

IT'S OKAY, PETER--

AND SO THEY RUSH FORWARD--

--INTO THE UNKNOWN.

THEY DO WHAT THEY BELIEVE THEY MUST.

THIS IS THE NATURE OF FAITH.

DON'T BE AN *IDIOT*, MARY JANE! STOP *STRUGGLING*!

YOU'LL KILL US *BOTH*!

THEN LET ME GO!

I WILL....*I WILL*....JUST AS SOON AS WE ARRIVE AT OUR *DESTINATION*.

WHERE, HARRY? WHERE ARE YOU *TAKING*--

OH NO!

YOU *REMEMBER*, DON'T YOU?

HOW COULD YOU... HOW COULD *ANY* OF US,...EVER *FORGET*?

THE PLACE WHERE ALL OUR HEARTS WERE FOREVER BROKEN...ALL OUR LIVES FOREVER *SHATTERED*. THE PLACE--

--WHERE *GWEN STACY* DIED!!

THIS IS THE *VERY SPOT* WHERE IT HAPPENED. SHE FELL... AND, IN A SENSE--

--WE *ALL* FELL *WITH* HER.

YOU UNDER-STAND, DON'T YOU, MARY JANE...WHY I HAD TO *BRING* YOU HERE?

YES...I UNDER-STAND.

AND I JUST WANT YOU TO KNOW-- THAT YOU'RE NOT GOING TO GET ANY BEGGING OR PLEADING FROM ME. I WON'T GIVE YOU THE *SATISFACTION.*

SO JUST *DO IT!*

I... I'M NOT *AFRAID* TO DIE.

DIE?!

MARY JANE--

--HOW COULD YOU EVEN *SAY* SUCH A THING?

I'D *NEVER* HURT YOU! *NEVER!*

YOU'RE MY *FRIEND...* ONE OF THE DEAREST FRIENDS I'VE EVER HAD!

I *LOVE* YOU!

YOU'VE SURE GOT A FUNNY WAY OF *SHOWING* IT.

NO, M.J.--NO! WHAT YOU'RE THINKING--! I *SWEAR* TO YOU...I WOULDN'T *DREAM* OF--

WHAT?

OH, I'M SO SORRY. I DIDN'T MEAN TO SCARE YOU LIKE THIS! I JUST WANTED TO--

YOU KNOW ...I STILL *MISS* GWEN. SO MUCH.

THERE ARE TIMES... EVEN AFTER ALL THESE YEARS...WHEN I JUST CAN'T BELIEVE IT. "IT CAN'T BE TRUE," I THINK. "SHE CAN'T REALLY BE DEAD."

AND WHEN I THINK OF HOW MY *FATHER* WAS *INVOLVED* IN IT, I--

"*INVOLVED*"--?! NORMAN OSBORN WASN'T "IN-VOLVED," HARRY! HE *KILLED* GWEN! *HE KILLED HER!*

HE *DID* *NOT!*

IT WAS A *SETUP!* YOUR STINKING *HUSBAND* SET HIM *UP!* HE--

H, WHAT'S THE POINT? YOU'LL NEVER *BELIEVE* E. YOU THINK PETER'S SOME... SAINT. PETER THE PERFECT. PETER THE GOOD.

NOTHING I SAY CAN CON-VINCE YOU HOW HE *CHANGES*-- WHEN HE PUTS ON THAT *MASK*--THAT *COSTUME*--!

HARRY--

--WHY DID YOU *BRING* ME HERE?

TO LET YOU KNOW THAT IT WILL *NEVER* COME TO THIS! WHAT HAPPENED WITH *GWEN*...I COULDN'T... I JUST...

MARY JANE, I *SWEAR!* YOU'VE GOT TO--

YOU REALLY *MEAN* IT, DON'T YOU?

WITH ALL MY HEART.

REMEMBER WHAT IT WAS LIKE...IN THE *OLD DAYS?* THOSE LONG, LAZY NIGHTS... JUST DRIVING AROUND TOGETHER? YOU, ME, GWEN... AND PETER.

THE ONLY THING ON OUR MINDS WAS HOW MUCH *FUN* WE COULD SQUEEZE INTO THE DAY...WHICH *DISCO* TO GO TO NEXT--

SO YOUNG, WEREN'T WE? SO INNOCENT.

YOUNG? SURE. INNOCENT? I DON'T KNOW.

WE WERE TRYING MIGHTY HARD TO *BE* INNOCENT. BUT WE ALL HAD OUR *PAIN,* HARRY, NO MATTER HOW MUCH WE TRIED TO *HIDE* IT.

MY FAMILY WAS A DYSFUNCTIONAL WRECK... PETER, ORPHANED, HIS UNCLE MURDERED--

--AND YOU--

YOUR MOTHER DEAD...AND YOUR *FATHER*--

DON'T YOU *TALK* ABOUT MY--

NO MATTER WHAT HAPPENS BETWEEN THE GREEN GOBLIN AND SPIDER-MAN... I WANT YOU TO KNOW THAT YOU'RE *SAFE.*

I LOVE YOU, MARY JANE. PETER'S *AUNT,* TOO. YOU'RE BOTH *FAMILY.* I'D DO *ANYTHING* FOR YOU.

THEN TAKE ME *HOME,* HARRY.

--BUT I'M AFRAID YOU'RE ALREADY *TOO LATE.*

WEB-HEADS!

Before we get to the usual nonsense, we wanted to take a moment to talk about something serious. As you read in the pages of this issue, the Kindred-resurrected Sin-Eater turned his mystically powered shotgun on himself. Even though this is a story about a very strange and fantastical villain, suicide is a very real subject and not one to gloss over. We wanted to make sure that it was clear that we weren't glorifying or in any way endorsing Sin-Eater's method of solving his problems. Suicide is not the answer to any problem, no matter how huge that problem is. If you are struggling with thoughts of suicide or are worried about a friend or loved one, please reach out to a counselor or someone you trust, call your local helpline, or call the National Suicide Prevention Lifeline: 1-800-273-8255.

Anyway, this epic yarn is nearing its end! Spider-Man is face-to-face with Kindred and Mary Jane is on her way to both of them! The other Spiders have been taken by Kindred as well, and who knows what further plans that centipedal villain has in store for them. Add Kingpin and Norman Osborn to that mix and you know you've got a classic Spider-Man story in the making. Nick Spencer (with Matthew Rosenberg) has been working his butt off to make this the biggest and best story possible, and Patrick Gleason, Mark Bagley, Marcelo Ferreira, Federico Vicentini, and Takeshi Miyazawa have crafted some of the most mind-bending visuals in the history of comics, so we hope your minds have been suitably bent.

And wasn't it great to see those pages from PETER PARKER: THE SPECTACULAR SPIDER-MAN #200?! You can thank Nick Spencer for its wonderful inclusion here, but thank J.M. DeMatteis for writing it, Sal Buscema for drawing it, Joe Rosen for lettering it, Bob Sharen for coloring it and Rob Tokar for editing it! We're super grateful in the Spider-Office as it's one of our faves!

Join us next week for the last AMAZING SPIDER-MAN issue of this crazy year and the climax of LAST REMAINS!

Keep Swinging!

Nick Lowe
Astoria, NY
November 17, 2020

#53.LR VARIANT BY
KHOI PHAM

#54.LR VARIANT BY
MARK BAGLEY, JOHN DELL & JASON KEITH